...remarkable
unique
magnificent
possible
evolutionary
unparalleled
powerful
beautiful
important
radiant
good enough
needed
badass
worth it
treasured
magical
imperfectly perfect
valued
legendary
rare

First Printing, 2017

Book ISBN: 978-0692951774

Book Cover & Interior Designed by Sally Morrow
Cover Illustrated by Martha Rich
Book Edited by Stephanie Rosic & Jen Johnson

———

i dedicate this book to
the best version of all of us
waiting to be discovered.

———

i gift this book to you,

every message within these pages are truths i wish i could tell you face to face. i wish i could be your reflection reminding you how your body is beautiful enough. i wish i could be your teammate reminding you of just how capable you are. i wish i could be your heart reminding you to give yourself room to love, care for, and be there for yourself. i wish i could be all these things and more. because i can't, my book is my substitute. let my stories tell you, you are not alone. let my words fill you with a sense of confidence.

this book is meant to lift you up and help you become the best version of yourself. this book is not a guide, but simply a collection of messages for you to interpret. in these pages, may you find something you resonate with and can keep with you.

may you leave this book (and come back) feeling confident, beautiful, and worth it. take what you read and live it out. may this book empower you to use your story and voice to inspire other girls.

but most important of all, may this gift make you smile.

love, J

———

it is time.
arise.

let this be your starting place

i'm a teenager so i get struggle. you know the phrase "fake it 'til you make it?" well i put my "fake" confidence in all the wrong things and truly never made it anywhere. i did many self-damaging things in order to fit in and have others accept me. i allowed too many people to walk all over me. i had one too many nights of crying myself to sleep over people who never cared for me. to be honest, i felt damaged.

thankfully i am not the same girl i used to be. i am now a beautiful work in progress. not perfect, but with everything i've learned, i've made it my goal to help other teenagers and young adults get through the same self-damaging things i went through.

i believe that everyone is a little broken and that is what makes us beautiful works in progress. we are all changing, growing, and being molded into better versions of ourselves; but we need a starting place. we need a place where we can accept our flaws and begin the process of learning self-love—a place to let go of self-hatred and regain self-confidence. think of this place as the beginning of the race in becoming the best version of who we are. it's a lifelong race, but don't be discouraged, because with every step we gain strength, courage, and wisdom. the goal is not to become perfect, but to simply become better than who we were yesterday. this is a race against our own fears, self-doubts, and struggles. if you have not already started this journey of self-love, allow this book to be your starting place. start here. keep reading and let every page be the next step you take in loving yourself more unconditionally and believing in yourself more than you ever have. start here. start now.

in the next pages, i have included various encouraging snippets of blog entries i wrote over the last two years. i wrote these words to inspire confidence in myself and other girls struggling with loving themselves. i hope these messages resonate with and encourage you. one thing i hope you hear each time you read this book is that you are 100 percent worth it—your life is worth living, your goals are worth pursuing, your story is valuable, and you are worth believing in. everything about you is worth more than you could ever imagine.

My Rock Bottom

14 years old,
I sit on the floor of my room with a bottle of weight loss pills.
I hate my body.
I want to be thin.
These pills are bound to get me there.

I do the math,
There are 50 pills so if I take two a day
I will have a "perfect body" in a month.
So with tears in my eyes,
I opened the lid and take two of them out.
I tell myself that if there isn't fast enough progress I can take
up to 3 or 4 of them a day to speed the process.

I sit back,
Shame, fear, and confusion fill my mind.
Mad at my body.
Scared about taking the pills.
Confused about everything else.
Why can't I just look like the other girls in my school?
Why am I taking pills? Because your body is fat, that is why.
Questions kept coming.

Head pounding,
I hit the floor.
I hit rock bottom.
I cannot take the pain anymore.
I let go of everything.
I let go of every belief I have about my body.
I let go of every question I have.

From my heart I hear:
You Are Beautiful.
Just the way you are.
It echoes through me.
It liberates me.

No, I am not thin like her, but I AM Beautiful.
No, I do not have straight hair like her, but I AM Beautiful.
No, I do not have light skin like her, but still I AM Beautiful.

Beautiful, Beautiful, Beautiful.
What did that word mean?
At the moment, I don't exactly know.
All I know is that this word allows me to let go
of everything I'm trying to be
And accept myself for who I am: beautiful.

I still remember that night as if it were yesterday.
That was the day I decided to make a change.
A change I never thought possible;
Learn to love myself the way I was.

From then on,
I surrounded myself with things that made me feel confident.
I found quotes about inner beauty, self-esteem, and acceptance.
Wrote them down over and over again.
Allowing each quote to ingrain itself in me.

I taped up positive messages all over my room.
I got rid of my magazines that only show stick thin models
And replaced them with positive messages.

Learning to love, accept, and call myself beautiful is a journey.
I am still on this journey.
Are you?

If so, let me be your positive message.
Let my words empower you.
You Are Beautiful.
You Are Beautiful.
You Are Beautiful.
...just the way you are.

outer beauty
-you are rockin' it girl!

her dimensions did not fit into beauty,
so what did she do?
she stretched the hell out of beauty,
until it was able to fit her too.

she wished for beauty,
her Creator granted her wish,
but when she looked back into the mirror,
nothing changed.

dear you,
there is no need to inject yourself
with their definition of beauty,
or carve your identity into
their standard of perfection.
do not let them sell you their false beauty
at the cost of who you are.

i am,
repeat after me

"i am beautiful just the way i am."
my body is beautiful.
my mind is beautiful.
my heart and soul are beautiful.
i am beautiful because i simply am.
the world may tell me i'm not,
but i have the power to create
my own definition of beautiful
and include myself in it.

"i am perfectly imperfect."
flaws and all,
i am my own one of a kind beautiful.
i am imperfect,
that's what makes me a perfect human.

"*i am unique for a reason.*"
i celebrate my uniqueness
because it sets me apart from the rest.
i am original,
the real deal.
there is only one me on this planet
and that is my superpower.

"*i define who i am, no one else.*"
they have their opinions of me,
but it does not change who i am,
i get to define who i am.
labels may try and diminish me,
but my worth will not be limited by them.
i am me:
whoever i choose to be.

her cracks stuck out,
her scars showed,
she was a beautiful
sculpture of brokenness.

don't call me "sexy,"
unless you are referring to
my mind, dreams, and ambitions.

sorry *not sorry*
i will not apologize
for loving myself.

*inspired by emily greener

beauty is multidimensional.
she comes in all shapes and shades.

want to feel more beautiful?
me too.

wear clothes that express what you love about yourself
wear clothes that make you feel confident, beautiful,
and powerful.
whether that may be a cute dress with flats,
or big sweatshirts and yoga pants, like me :)
wear what you want to wear,
do your own thang!

sing empowering songs in the shower
i hope i'm not the only one who sings in the shower.
now, i don't have the greatest voice,
but singing my favorite empowering songs
helps boost my confidence.
if you haven't tried it, you must.
go find some empowering songs and
rock out to them.
...besides, why not?

write yourself mini letters
all you do is write yourself a very sweet letter.
make sure to describe yourself as amazing,
impactful, gorgeous, and other positive things.
once you are done writing them,
place them in random places:
like your jacket pocket, your junk drawer,
your backpack, purse, etc.
then go on about your day.
whenever you come across the letters
they will stand as little reminders
of how wonderful you are!

fill the space you occupy in this world.
it's yours.
all of it.
don't rob yourself of it
by trying to become someone else.

do not be fooled by
her beauty, her softness.
she is no ordinary princess,
she is a *queen* who saved
her own damn self.

if only you could see yourself
from my perspective;
your sparkly eyes,
your vibrant smile.
you would finally understand why you are
so undeniably beautiful.
-love, your reflection

trends about beauty that will
never define you

so called "fruit" shape
ever heard of the "fruit body shape" rules?
like if you have an apple shape don't wear this,
or if you have a pear shape you can wear this.
please—(*major eye roll*)
you can wear whatever the heck you want to wear.
those rules are dumb, so forget about them.
do your own thing and love yourself for it.

whether you have a thigh gap or not
now, i am not hating on anyone who has a thigh gap,
i'm just saying that this should not determine
if you are attractive or not.
you have to be born with the thigh gap
in order to have one,
you cannot just get one.
so if you were not born with it, like me,
then relax and accept the way your body is.
all girls—thigh gap or not—are beautiful.
don't let society trick you all up.

the size of your waist, thighs, hips—aka body
you don't have to be a size 0
to be considered a model,
and you shouldn't be called a plus size model
if you have a regular sized healthy body.
your size is your size.
that's it.
not a measurement of your worth,
value, or importance.
just a number that people obsess over too much.
you are beautiful.
period.

dressing sexy isn't an exploitation of my body,
it's a manifestation of my confidence.

"you're pretty ~~for a black girl.~~"

no. i'm just pretty.
thank you.
-anonymous

makeup should be an accessory,
not an identity.
love your natural self too.

i'm fat.
no, wrong spelling:
*i'm fab.
-anonymous

supposed to do
a turtle could hate itself because of its huge shell,
a chameleon could hate itself because of its
camouflaging skin,
a giraffe could hate itself because of its long neck.
but that would be ridiculous, right?
so why do you hate yourself for having
the body you have?
your body is meant to protect you and keep you alive.
that is why it is naturally beautiful,
because it does what it is supposed to do.

inner beauty

-i mean, have you seen your
heart, it's breathtaking!

harvest of beauty
beauty sprouts from her soul,
not the beauty you find in magazines,
the beauty only the heart can manifest:
her harvest of love.

you are so much more than just beautiful
—beauty is more than skin deep

be compassionate—help others
yes, you are beautiful on the outside,
yet, your loving and compassionate heart
is even more breathtaking.
let your heart be the thing
you keep trying to improve,
not just your waistline.

be dedicated—make an impact
why just be beautiful,
when you can be beautiful and dedicated?
persevere,
go after your goals and don't give up.
yes, this is a lot easier said than done,
but it's worth it.
others will see your hard work,
be inspired by you and go after their own dreams.

be intelligent—be "pretty" smart
this world already has beautiful girls,
what it needs are more smart and powerful girls.
so go be remembered for your power,
dedication, and compassion for others.
impress people with your brilliance,
not your new makeup.

you have so many undiscovered
treasures within you.
dig honey, dig.
your riches are worth discovering.

one piece of advice every girl
needs to hear

you are enough
if you didn't catch that,
you are enough.
you don't have to have a "perfect" body to be enough.
you don't need to get all "a's" in order to be enough.
nope, you are already enough,
just the way you are.
what makes you enough does not lie
in your accomplishments or
what you look like.
it lies in the simple fact that you are human.
you are imperfect.
maybe even a little broken.
that's ok.
you are *still* enough.

tú eres la definición de belleza.
you are the definition of beauty.

beauty
beauty is soul deep.
be beautifully brave.
be beautifully heroic.
be beautifully powerful.
be beautiful.
be you.

your heart's beauty
no petal on a flower is perfectly formed,
yet, that does not stop the world
from admiring them.
so why question your formation?
it's not about your body's dimensions,
it's about the beauty your heart brings to this world.

you're an ocean of endless beauty
she stood in front of the ocean,
in awe of its endless depth of unknown majesty.
the ocean gazed back at her,
in awe of her endless depth of unknown beauty.

You Can't Find Confidence

I got an F.
I failed math.
Junior year, First Semester.
It really hurt.
More like excruciating.

Math was my strongest subject.
Key word: was.
I excelled in math.
Reached the 2nd highest math in my school:
IB Math High Level 1.

I tried my best,
Studied hard.
But no matter how hard I tried,
I still failed.
My learning style did not correlate
to my teacher's teaching style.

I became a failure.
Forget my other A's and one B.
They didn't matter.
What mattered was that I was no longer perfect.
I was imperfect.

I let my confidence depend on my grades.
That was the problem.
You can't find confidence in grades or success.
You must simply be confident.

If you feel that you have to go out in the world
and find your worth or sense of confidence,
You are looking in the wrong place.
You are what you are looking for.
You have the confidence within,
You just haven't allowed yourself
to discover that treasure yet.
Stop searching for things and start being.
Be confident.
Believe in yourself.
Love yourself.

withstanding negativity
-they may label you, but you are
the one who gets to define you!

their inability to see your greatness,
is not because you lack greatness,
it is because they are blinded
by their own doubt.

stop beating yourself up for
making mistakes

they shape you into someone better
the first thing we need to realize is
that making mistakes is inevitable.
that said, they are also helpful.
with mistakes comes the chance
to learn something new
or appreciate something more than we did before.
mistakes are here for a purpose;
to help make you into a better you.
so stop getting so worked up over your mistake.
chill out, girl.
instead use that mistake to improve yourself.

they lay in the past, now it's time to let them go
mistakes are meant to guide you,
not define you.
once you've learned from them,
let them go.
it's ok to reflect on your mistakes,
to see how far you have come.
just don't keep replaying your mistakes in your head,
forgive yourself.
ask for forgiveness from others if you have to,
and move on.

"if 'plan a' went wrong, don't worry, there are 25 other letters in the alphabet keep cool" -unknown

whether it's your 1st mistake or 290,384th,
no matter what number it is,
there is an infinite amount of opportunities
for you to get something right.
just keep trying.
plus, side note:
no human is expected to get everything right
on their first try
...and that includes you.

vulnerability is not weakness
sharing your story with the world takes courage.
owning your mistakes takes humility.
speaking your truth takes bravery.
admitting you're wrong takes guts.
vulnerability is not weakness.
it takes your greatest strength to show
your biggest weakness.

*inspired by alexis jones

i don't need your applause,
i have two hands and can clap for myself.

tell me, love,
when will you stop letting them define you?

their words weakened her,
their opinions broke her.
but they only weakened her fear,
and only broke her silence.
from their hatred arose her voice.

dear me
they said i would lose, but i've already won.
they said it would be impossible,
but i've already accomplished it.
they said many things, but i've defied them all.
their words didn't limit me.
their opinions didn't define me.
their disbelief didn't hinder me.
you were a winner from the start.
believe in yourself.
-future self

your hope can light up even
the darkest places,
your love can pierce through
even the hardest hearts,
your voice can shift
even the loudest opinions.
do not underestimate your power.

the best way to knock down your confidence is
by comparing yourself to someone else.
we are all on our own paths;
there is no need for comparison.

believing in yourself
-you got this! now go for it!

awake.
your power has been
dormant for far too long.

do you wish to become
confident?
powerful?
legendary?
then be confident.
be powerful.
be legendary.
you cannot become
until you decide to be.

girl power looks like owning your femininity while still rocking your assertive and ambitious sides.

shimmer, darling, shimmer.

confidence is the radical idea
of believing in yourself.

ponder this as you start your day
how can i be the best me today?
is there any emotional baggage that i should let go?
what can i do today that tomorrow will thank me for?
how can i expand my comfort zone?
how will i celebrate myself today?
what can i do to make someone else's day?

you sparkle,
even on your dullest days.

it's one thing to say that you're confident.
it's another thing to embody it
even when you don't feel confident.

speak your truth unapologetically
—because your voice
is your greatest power

"i am beautiful!"
go ahead, say it.
we spend too much time
whispering to ourselves
all of our imperfections.
it's time to start shouting out
compliments about what
makes us beautiful.

"i'm sorry."
own your mistakes.
say sorry.
ask for forgiveness.
and
forgive yourself.

"i'm awesome!"
when was the last time you told yourself,
"i'm awesome!"
we all do amazing things every day,
so take time to recognize every time you succeed.
even the little successes.
they are worth celebrating.
because they motivate you to keep going
and believe in yourself.

"*i deserve more than this.*"
never settle for less than what
you believe you deserve.
you are worth way too much.

"no, thanks."
no one ever said you had to
say "yes" to everything.
if you don't want it, say no.
it's not rude,
it's not bitchy,
it's just you not wanting
what others have to offer.
...and that is perfectly fine.
no need to explain yourself,
you don't owe anyone that.

"*i messed up.*"
when you make a mistake,
it's okay to admit it.
we are all human,
so cut yourself some slack,
get up and try again.

"today is just not my day."
if it is not your day,
then it's not your day.
i know as much as we are
"supposed to" live life to the fullest
and never take any moment for granted,
there will always be days when we
just aren't feeling very optimistic.
it's ok if you don't want to smile or laugh,
who said you had to?

"*this is me, accept it or leave it!*"
some people won't approve of your decisions,
or who you've become.
but, hey, who said we wanted
their approval (in the first place)?
be you. do you.
if they don't like you,
that's their problem.

proudly be yourself
-embrace your true colors, it is what
makes this world beautiful

love your weirdness
we are all weird in our own unique way,
whether it's our laugh,
the faces we make,
our secret talents, and habits.
own and love your weirdness
because you wouldn't be you without it.

learn to embrace being different
you and i are very different,
that's what makes us so beautiful.
you have your unique features and i have mine.
every one of us is a one-in-a-lifetime-kind-of-girl.
so embrace that fact.

be proud of yourself.
celebrate yourself.
...it means more cake ;)

My BFF's: Me, Myself, and I

Ever walked past someone you've talked to and watched them ignore you?
Ever waved at someone and watched them look down at their phone?
Ever felt lonely in a whole crowd of people?
Ever thought you would end up "forever alone?"
I have.

After losing so many friends I taught myself to hate being alone.
I saw it as something bad.
Alone meant feeling empty and being left behind.

But now I know that even when I am physically alone,
I don't have to be lonely.
It simply means that no one is by your side.
You cannot control who stays by your side,
but you can dictate how you feel about being alone.
You can either let it bring you to tears
or allow it to help you gain independence.

The world has taught us that in order to be "cool"
you have to have a crowd of people standing around.
But remember that the greatest accomplishers in the world
were the ones who went against the current,
left the crowd, and became comfortable standing alone.

I've learned to be content by myself and accept the fact that
people will treat me the way they treat themselves.
People who respect themselves will respect others.
People who hate themselves will try and pull you down
so they can feel better.
Learning this helped me realize that the horrible way I was treated
reflected more about who they were
than who I was.

I've also learned to enjoy my own company
and become best friends with myself.
I've taught myself self-love, along with self-care and self-appreciation.
So yes, my BFF's are me, myself, and I.
It's OK to be friends with yourself.
You should be friends with yourself!

You can't truly love others if you don't first love yourself.
In order to have the best relationships with others,
you first must have a healthy relationship with yourself.
Having a solid relationship with yourself will help you create future
relationships with others,
leave dead-end relationships, and fix broken ones.
So be your own best friend, girl.
You are an amazing person, so get to know yourself!

relationship with yourself
—'cause being besties with
yourself should be cool!

your relationship with yourself
is the most important.
invest in it.

i asked myself out,
i said "yes."
it's been happy ever after since.

be your own best friend
—because what better friend to have
than yourself?

who else knows you better than you know yourself?
yes, you can go to your friends
for help, advice, or motivation.
but it is you in the end
who makes the final decision.
either to accept their advice or take your own.
only you know what you truly need.
your body is your body,
your mind is your mind,
and your heart is your heart.
so don't be afraid to turn to yourself
in a time of need.

friends will come and go, but you've got you for life.
friendships will come and go.
but you do have a friend that will
never leave your side.
you just have to let them be your friend.
you have to learn to listen to yourself,
take your own advice,
motivate yourself,
and comfort yourself.
never leave yourself hanging,
lift yourself up and
keep moving forward.

you deserve your own kindness.
you deserve the same love and care
you show towards others.
you are deserving of kindness,
respect, and dignity;
especially from yourself.

it's your job to love yourself, no one else's.
it is your job to understand your worth,
and not wait for others to realize your worth.
it is your job to love yourself,
not wait for others to love you.
it is your job to give yourself what you want.
there is no harm in asking for help,
but you should never solely depend on someone
to give you what you can get yourself.

honestly, it's cool to be besties with yourself.
you may think being your own bestie is weird,
because "what will others think?"
but trust me,
once you create a loving relationship with yourself,
their opinions of you won't matter;
your validation will come from within.

treat yourself the way you would
want your best friend to treat herself.

the love you seek in others is waiting to be
discovered within your own heart.
love yourself.

relationship with others
-some friendships are
awesome while others
are better left alone.

love is holding onto people
despite our differences,
hate is pushing away people
because of our differences.

gratitude is best expressed
"actions speak louder than words"
—anonymous

be there for her:
it may be giving her a huge bear hug,
a sincere note, a coffee date,
or whatever she likes best.
whatever you choose,
make sure to be there for her when she needs it.
being present is the best gift you can give her.

forgive her:
disputes happen and feelings get hurt.
but if you learn to forgive quickly,
things can clean up faster.
so if she hurts your feelings,
forgive her and move on.
no point in holding grudges,
they get you nowhere.

motivate & support her:
if your bestie has a big project coming up,
motivate her to do her best.
if she just got out of a hard relationship,
comfort her and help her gain her confidence back.
do whatever you can to support her.

respect her:
both you and your bestie are two different people
and are bound to have differences.
respect your differences.
you may have different beliefs, styles, and opinions;
you need to respect that.

*whenever I see a girl feeling down

"hey babe,
you forgot your crown."
—anonymous

compliment her
like her shoes?
think her hair looks on point?
diggin' her outfit?
...then compliment her.

impressed by her skills?
loving her ideas?
inspired by her leadership?
...then let her know.

celebrate each other more.
it's honestly not that hard.

hurt people hurt people
she backstabbed you,
she spread rumors about you,
she even took your best friend away.
but did it ever occur to you,
the pain she caused you did not
compare to the pain she caused herself?
the rumors she spread about you did not
compare to the things she called herself?
the loneliness she gave you did not
compare to the loneliness she felt herself?
people treat themselves ten times worse
than the way they treat you.
their quickest way to release pain is
to pass it on to others.
hurt people hurt people.
so keep spreading love,
even to those who you
believe don't deserve it.
love is the cure for pain.

inspired by "i am that girl"

jealousy is inferior,
you are above that level.

train yourself to see the best in others,
because just like them,
the best version of you should
shine brighter than your flaws.

celebrate other girls
if she tries to pull you down,
elevate her.
if she tries to tear you apart,
empower her.
even if she tries to destroy your life,
celebrate her.
because lowering down to her level
won't help you rise.
want to win?
lift her up.

relationships with lovers
-promise me you'll never
settle for anything less
than what you deserve!

"why would anyone ever
want to date me?"
well here are some reasons why

because you are beautiful
you are beautiful my love,
with your beautiful smile,
and unmistakable gorgeous eyes.
do not for a second think you are ugly
because your crush never complimented you.
their said or unsaid opinions of you do not
determine if you are beautiful or not.
you just are.

because you are unique
you are like no other on this planet
and that is something to be proud of.
do not think that you have to be like another girl
in order to get the attention you want.
be different.
stand out.
there is enough copying in this world,
do your own thing.

because you are talented
the skills and talents you have are
what make you, you,
do not second guess them.
just because others did not notice
your abilities and strengths
does not mean they aren't there.

because you are smart
all of your ideas, life experiences, and perspectives
give into the knowledge you possess.
please never be that girl who dumbs herself down
in front of others to get their attention.
don't be afraid to be smart.
smart girls rock!
be real, never fake.

because you are worth everything
anyone would be lucky to get you,
blessed in fact.
you are worthy of the best
and i hope you never cheat yourself of that
by questioning your importance.
love yourself,
because single or not,
you are amazing!

she offered him her heart,
but he left her in search of the world,
not realizing she was a universe.

gifts every girl deserves on her first (or next) date
the gift of kindness,
the gift of respect,
the gift of importance,
the gift of honesty,
the gift of love,
...and always dessert!

tears are your heart's way of speaking.
listen.

he beat her with all his might,
but was unable to break her.
bones break and skin bleeds,
but her love for herself kept her whole.

there is a difference between being
alone and feeling lonely:
you don't need to be alone to feel lonely,
but you don't have to feel lonely
when you are alone.

he mistook me for being gentle,
so he tried to take advantage of me.
then he met the lion in me.

live happily ever after
even if you are single
be your own prince

don't let your happiness depend on your status.
when we attach our happiness to other things like
relationships, money, fame, etc.
it becomes dependent on those things,
which are unreliable.
happiness is a state of mind.
it is a decision;
choose wisely my friend.

do things that make you happy.
do the things you love.
what are you passionate about?
what makes your heart light up?
you can still live a full and successful life single.
take risks and try new things.
stop waiting for a relationship to live your life.
live *now.*

stop thinking you are worthless because you are single.
too many of us have ingrained in ourselves
that we will only be valuable once
someone falls in love with us.
but that is bull.
you are worth more than you could ever imagine,
and your value will never,
and i mean never,
depend on whether you are in a relationship or not.

treat yourself right.
buy yourself some flowers,
give yourself compliments,
wink at yourself in the mirror.
don't wait for someone to take you to dinner,
take yourself,
that way, you won't have to share your food :)

understand *the importance of singlehood.*
the truth is being single is important.
this is the time where you can learn about yourself
and begin to grow into who you want to become.
this time allows you to slow down,
listen to your inner voice,
and find your passions.
don't take this time for granted
and don't hate it either.
it can be tough,
but it is worth it.

bathe with flowers,
eat a whole cake by yourself,
do whatever you need to do
to deal with the pain.

Setting Goals Vs. Accomplishing Goals

The ratio between the goals I've set and
the goals I've accomplished are a little offset.
I have no problem setting them,
the issue comes when trying to accomplish them.

For example, I've always had this goal to work out more and eat healthy.
Whenever I set out to do this, I start out strong.
I look up many ab, leg, and arm toning workouts,
I print workouts that gradually get harder over the weeks,
I make incentives,
and even create healthy meals.
In other words, I go ALL out.

So as you can imagine,
week one goes just as planned.
Week two on the other hand does not.
My excitement disappears.
I burn out.
I put all of my printouts into a binder
and put it back on my shelf to collect dust.

So there you have it.
Another goal not accomplished.
But why?
Why am I able to work successfully toward some of my goals
and not others?

There is a huge difference between setting goals and actually
accomplishing them.
We may wish we could achieve goals as fast as we came up with them,
but it doesn't work like that.
I learned this, of course, the hard way.

I still have that binder with all of the workouts and meal plans,
and whenever I glance over at it, I simply laugh.
Like girl, what were you thinking?

Going all out like that was bound to end in burn out.
It's important to push yourself,
but it's more important to create balance.

This applies to any goal.
For any goal you set,
go steady and strong.
Push yourself and take needed breaks.
Allow yourself to take it slow,
because even the tortoise reached the finish line faster than the hare.
The tortoise paced itself but the hare burned out.

You are a work in progress,
so give yourself enough time and space to progress.

step into the unbelievable,
dance in the unpredictable,
live in the impossible.

we need more female badasses.
be the next one.

be a dreamer.
be an empowerer.
be a world changer.

you become unstoppable
once you realize your full potential.

no dream is yours;
it belongs to whoever is
brave enough to go after it.

breathe.
breathe.
in and out.
feel that?
that's the feeling of possibility.
listen to your heartbeat.
listen again.
hear that?
that's the sound of purpose.

give your dreams a chance,
even if they seem impossible.
you are worth the possibility
of them coming true.

take risks.
you are capable of so much more
than you think!

expand your comfort zone
there are many kinds of risks;
going somewhere new,
meeting new people,
and learning a new language.
stepping out of your bubble and
experiencing the world
will help expand your comfort zone and
make you a well-rounded person.
if you want to live your life to the fullest,
you must go out and actually live.

get over your fears
are you afraid of getting hurt?
messing up?
or actually succeeding?
you cannot let fear hold you back
from living a life of purpose.
yes, you will mess up and get a little dirty,
but that is what life is all about.
it's about falling down and getting back up stronger.
it's about doing what you love,
no matter what lies ahead!

find out who you are
taking risks helps you discover
new things about yourself.
if you never dip your toes into different things,
how will you know if you like them or not?
it's kind of like being at a buffet with a variety of food.
if you don't try at least one bite,
how will you know if you like it?
you may try it and hate it,
or you may try it and love it, who knows?
go out and discover yourself.

inspire others to take risks
when you step out of your comfort zone
and try something new,
others will be impacted by your bravery.
some will still call you crazy,
but others will be encouraged and
start taking risks themselves.
so show others how it's done,
go out and live fearless by
taking healthy and meaningful risks.

define your goal.
refine your plan.
redefine the impossible.

you'll slip, trip, and most definitely fall.
the question though, is *will you get back up?*

the sky is not your limit
your mind is your limit.
what you believe is possible is your limit.
what you believe you are capable of is your limit.
what you believe is tangible is your limit.
you are your only limit.
you are also limitless.

get off your cute ass and
make some magic!

don't just be a leader,
be a creator of leaders.
help others find their own
strength, potential, and power.

*inspired by tricia buell

i'll become so powerful,
i won't be breaking through glass ceilings,
i'll be stepping on them.

every girl has the power
to reach her dreams.
dreams are illustrations of your potential.

you were born with a purpose
darling, you were not placed on this earth for nothing.
you were born with a purpose,
specifically assigned to you.
your dreams aren't meant to stay as dreams,
they are meant to be accomplished.
so wake up,
get up,
and go after them.

you have your own set of gifts
you may think that you will never reach your dreams
because you don't have any 'talents.'
but you must understand that we all have a gift
to give to this world.
even if your gift may seem insignificant (to yourself
or others),
realize that when you use your gift to help others
that is when you become *powerful*.

use everything set against you as
"stepping stones to greatness"
-oprah winfrey

others will always try and dim your light
and try to stop you from reaching your dreams.
don't let them.
keep going.
use everything thrown at you
to make you stronger.

have confidence in your own abilities
no matter how many people stand against you,
they should never stop you from
pursuing your dreams.
their disbelief does not determine your capabilities.
so prove their butts wrong and do the unimaginable!
your dreams are possible.
you are possible.

...and then i finally asked myself,
"why wouldn't i be worth it?"

surprise yourself
impress yourself
outdo yourself

step into living
every step you take is your imprint on this earth.
climb the highest mountains,
challenge yourself.
swim the deepest seas,
surprise yourself.
travel the longest distances,
transform yourself.
do not contain your wonder,
experience.
live.
create the greatest story ever told.

you feel like quitting?
good.
that means you've tried your best.
now create a new "best"
and try again.

reflection of your light
the greatness you see in me,
lives inside of you.
the potential you've discovered in me,
waits to be discovered in you, by you.
the inspiration you feel beside me,
is the same inspiration i feel beside you.
i am simply a reflection of your light.
keep shining my bright star.

*inspired by camellia khalvati

she kept climbing until
the stars became her walkway.

trust your wings.

awaken the go-getter girl in you
because we are all badasses

make the decision
want to create your own business?
want to find the cure to cancer?
want to save animals?
then do it.
start small and grow.
but first,
say yes.

surround yourself with other go-getters
want to feel powerful and motivated?
then surround yourself with other go-getters
who are ready to make this world a better place.
the people you hang out with influence you,
so choose your peers wisely.

defriend self-doubt & befriend self-love
you can't let your girl boss come out
if you are constantly questioning yourself.
don't put yourself down.
learn to love yourself,
accept yourself,
and believe in yourself.
how do you do that?
get rid of all your negative talk
and replace it with encouragement.

write your goals down
for those out there who want to become go-getters,
you must have goals to go after.
once you have a goal,
write it down,
believe it's possible,
and start working at it.

give yourself some positive fuel
every go-getter needs encouragement.
if you ever start feeling worried, tired,
or on the edge of giving up, refuel yourself.
this fuel can be anything really,
it just has to make you feel powerful again.
it might be relaxing, having a dance party,
listening to powerful music,
or looking up inspirational quotes.
whatever it is,
make sure you have something.
do not give up.

your dreams are a manifestation
of our world's potential.

your power
it's that little voice that tells you, "yes i can!"
it's that spark of hope that stops you from giving up.
it's that last push of energy
that pushes you past the finish line.
that is where your power is.
it shows itself when you need it most.

let your success speak for itself.
invest in your roots and in due time
flowers will reveal themselves.

what i want to be
to be the smartest person is not my goal.
to be the most beautiful person is still not my goal.
to be the greatest person is not my goal.
to become my smartest self is my goal.
to become my most beautiful self is my goal.
to become my greatest self is my goal.
the best me is what i want to be.

fierceness glittered in her eyes.
nothing was going to stop her.

her heart left the world shook.

~~happy~~ ever after

You might be wondering why i crossed out the happy in "happy ever after."
I did it to show that a story doesn't have to end with this saying in order
to be a valid story. Some chapters of our lives don't end like this and
that's okay.

I still sometimes get up in the morning feeling less than beautiful. I still
struggle accepting that some jeans don't fit anymore. I still feel lonely
some days. I still have to remind myself that i'm not perfect and don't have
to be. I'm still fighting for my freedom to be able to love myself
unconditionally and live my life to the absolute fullest. So no, it's not a
"happy ever after," but it's still a story i am proud to call my own.

These pages are simply a snippet of my recent past that is setting me up
for a brighter future. There were a lot of ups and downs, just like there will
be in my future. My story is not finished yet. But today, this is where i set
my pen down and let everything speak for itself.

I hope that my story created a platform for you to both reflect upon and
tell your story. We each come with a unique past and shouldn't keep it to
ourselves. When we are brave enough to speak our truth and tell our
stories, we create space for others to say "me too" and tell their truths. The
more stories that are told, the more we as girls will realize that we are not
alone, that others struggle in similar ways, and that together we can
support and lift one another up.

Our pasts do not have the power to define our todays, but, help mold and
shape us into the person we will be in the future. If your past is darker than
most, don't be ashamed. You are the light at the end of the tunnel. You
survived whatever tried to break you. Keep hoping, keep loving, keep
striving, and keep allowing yourself to be a work in progress.

write your name in the lives you meet,
leave your lasting mark.
an inspiring mark.

pass on this gift

who in your life needs to hear these words? after you have ingrained these messages in your own heart and filled these pages with your own inspiring story, make sure to pass this book on to continue the 'me too' ripple effect.

From:

To:

I pass on this gift to you

_____

_____

_____

_____

_____

_____

_____

_____

_____

Love,

———

pass on this gift, again

who in your life needs to hear these words? after you have ingrained these messages in your own heart and filled these pages with your own inspiring story, make sure to pass this book on to continue the 'me too' ripple effect.

———

From:

To:

I pass on this gift to you

_____

_____

_____

_____

_____

_____

_____

_____

_____

_____

_____

Love,

Acknowledgement Page

It took much more than my own two hands to create this book. A village of passionate hearts and unbelievable talents brought this book to life. Here is to my Me Too village! Thank you.

My Inspirations
To the one who sparked this book idea in the first place, thank you mama for being right once again. Your suggestion of keeping my blog entries to use in the future, helped create a foundation on which I built Me Too. So once again, thank you. You not only planted the seed, but also continued watering and feeding this idea with your love, support, and faith in me.

Alexis Jones, from your written inspiration to your empowering organization I AM THAT GIRL, thank you for introducing me to what self-love looks like and helping me discover my own voice. Your mentorship through the years has taught me many things, perhaps the most important was learning how to own my story and use it to make this world better.

My Production Team
I could not have asked for a more passionate team than my Me Too Team. Each one of you made this all possible. I am humbled by your willingness to make my crazy ideas happen.

Lee Layne, you were the first person to say YES to joining my team. I am so grateful for your faith in me from the very beginning. You have mentored me, helped me with the legal side of publishing a book, and have always been there for me. Thank you.

Jen Johnson and Stephanie Rosic, thank you for helping me shape and mold my story into one that is grammatically correct. Your ability to tweak my sentences, while still allowing my voice to come through is incredible. So grateful for both your time and effort on Me Too.

Martha Rich, thank you for the beautiful cover design for Me Too. It perfectly encapsulates what Me Too stands for, as it incorporates unique, raw, and authentic art.

Sally & David Morrow, your creative talent is admirable. Thank you for volunteering your creativity to help design and produce Me Too; and Kristin Anderson who helped us with the production work. From your initial cover ideas to the final design of the interior to the production—Me Too would not have its authentic look and feel without you. Thank you!

Lindsay Robb, my marketing genius! Thank you girl for also jumping onto my crazy dream and giving me pointers on how to send this creation into the world. I am beyond grateful for your mentorship and friendship.

My Support System
Because I decided to self-publish, the process was more costly in the beginning. I want to take the time to thank every one of you who have helped finance Me Too. Thank you to my amazing parents; Amy & Eugene Brownell, Betty Bordner, Ann Brownell, Yana Engel, Granme & Gramps (Sylvia & Jim Kemp), Franca Bukowsky, Monique Whitcomb, Kate McCarthy, Susan Emery, Rich Kemp, Alisha Zhao, Olivia Gardner, Elaine Blok, David Rueck, Lee Layne, Kristen & Andrew Marshall, Vanessa Wood, Bobby Harris, Erica Lucas, Erin Jones, Sarah & James Stamper, Diana Ball, Laura Smith, Maria Dodson, Phillips Clan, Jennifer Blough, Rebecca Snyder, Kathy Costley-Sakona, Myra Huang, Johanna Stryker-Smit, Anika Nichols, Kelsae Stentzel, Maria McLaughlin, Dawn Watson, Liette Witherrite, Gerald Walle, the Hildebrandt family, Carla Perdiz, Monica Murphy, Mikerlange MacNicol, Eva Klijnhout, Mikal Shabazz, and all of the anonymous donors as well.

...and I can't forget those who were there for my moral support! Thank you to the rest of my incredible family. Thank you friends for your motivation. Thank you to everyone who has been a part of shaping me and my life. I am forever grateful for ALL of you.

———

more about me

i can't spell, but i LOVE to write. i believe anything is possible with enough faith. i am stubborn, but it helps me never give up on my dreams. i am a strong believer in love and justice. i like to think you can learn something new from everyone. i love listening to others stories. i am both a perfectionist and procrastinator—and no that is not a good mix. i have two names: the first is the one I go by, Jolie Brownell, and the second is my birth name, Venetine Virgile. i am adopted from Haiti, like all five of my siblings. i love my smile. i hope to travel more of the world someday. i find inspiration from everything and everyone—including you.

love, J